GRANDMOTHER EARTH XI:
2005

Old soldiers once young
Proudly marching flags held high
Freedom does not die.

Laurie Boulton

GRANDMOTHER EARTH XI: 2005

Patricia Smith
Frances Brinkley Cowden
Editors

Frances Darby
Marcelle Z. Nia
Mary Frances Broome
Editorial Assistants

Featuring
Award-winning
Poetry and Prose
from the

2004 GRANDMOTHER EARTH
NATIONAL WRITING CONTEST

GRANDMOTHER EARTH CREATIONS
Cordova, Tennessee

Cover Photo by Laurie Boulton
Annual Veterans Reunion in Melbourne, FL—raising flag before opening ceremonies, above the stage pavilion. The event draws about 100,000 one week each spring: veterans, family members and friends of veterans. The POW [Prisoner of War] black and white flag is then raised to fly beneath the American flag. Live music, speakers, booths of memorabilia, and most importantly a 7/8 scale of The [Viet Nam Memorial] Wall with over 58,000 names etched into the black granite. The photo is reprinted from Boulton's illustrated book, *Heart to Heart: Poetry for Veterans*, 1999. 2nd edition, revised, 2004. The book is given to veterans.
ISBN 1-884289-48-7   10.00

FIRST EDITION: 2005
GRANDMOTHER EARTH CREATIONS
P. O. Box 2018
Cordova, TN 38088
Phone: (901) 309-3692
gmoearth@aol.com
www.grandmotherearth.com

We hopefully will stop to consider
All the blessings we've had since birth;
One of the greatest God has provided
Is our home—Grandmother Earth.
--Embree Bolton

This edition is lovingly dedicated to the memory
of

Lourine White
Piggott, Arkansas
Poet and Friend to Poets

Grandmother Earth XI Winners

POETRY: Stephen Malin, Judge

1st   To My Mother, Maureen Cannon, Ridgewood, NJ
2nd   Set Free in Encrements, Eileen Malone, Colm, CA
3rd   Ultra Sounds, Margo LaGattuta, Rochester, MI
4th   Brain Dancing, Rosalyn Ostler, Salt Lake City, UT

Special Merit: Memories of a Divorce, to a Novice, Laura Black, Atlanta GA

Honorable Mention:
Roof of Flowers, Verna Lee Hinegardner, Hot Springs, AR
Desert Night Drifting, Kolette Montague, Centerville, UT
A World Apart, Frieda Beasley Dorris, Memphis, TN
The Barking, Clovita Rice, Little Rock, AR
Wolves of Winter, Charlene Villella, Murray UT

Bouquet to the Fallen, Lucille Morgan Wilson, Des
Moines, IA
Pot Holders, Jane Randall, Centerville, UT
Fox Hollow, Elizabeth Howard, Crossville, TN
Musings of the Mad Widow, Anna DeMay, Orange Park,
FL

HAIKU: Thomas McDaniel, Judge

1st   Sun-beaded dewdrops, Anne-Marie Legan,
Herrin, IL
1HM   a slim cat watches, Helen Allison, Memphis, TN
2HM   River iced over, Ellaraine Lockie, Sunnyvale, CA
3HM   Dropped from brown branches, Angela Logsdon,
Memphis, TN

SHORT FORM: Elaine Nunnally Davis, Judge

1st   Sky Trails, Tana Harwood Ford, Vicksburg, MS
1HM   Every Path, Laura Black, Atlanta, GA
2HM   Scent of Citrus, Marilyn Stacy, Dallas, TX
3HM   The Endless Beach, Lois Batchelor Howard,
Santee, CA

HUMOROUS POETRY: Dorothy Tacker, Judge

1st   Obedience, Lucy Ray, Memphis, TN
1HM   Growing Older, Helen Thomas Allison,
Memphis, TN
2HM   The Morning After, Ellaraine Lockie, Sunnyvale,
CA

ENVIRONMENTAL POETRY: Marcelle Nia, Judge

1st   Skipping Stars, Rhonda Roberts, Searcy, AR
HM   Waterfall, Stacy Smith, Anderson, IN
Woodland Mystery, Anne-Marie Legan, Herrin,
IL
I, the Mountain, Lois Batchelor Howard, Santee,
CA
Masterpiece, Pame Bosman, Bunnell, FL

PROSE: Dr. Malra Treece, Judge

1st	The Ages of Woman, Madge Lewis, Memphis, TN
2nd	When the Yellow Fever Came, Sarah Hull Gurley, Germantown, TN
3rd	Long Walk Home, Martha McNatt, Jackson, TN
1HM	The Table, Madge Lewis, Memphis, TN
2HM	Under the Oak, Malu Graham, Memphis, TN
3HM	Help Wanted, Sarah Hull Gurley, Germantown, TN
4HM	One Owner Antique Car, Marcia Camp, Little Rock, AR

ENVIRONMENTAL PROSE: Frances Cowden, Judge

1st	Otto, Olivia and Oscar…, Betty Gifford, Denver, CO

HUMOROUS PROSE: Louise Gerain, Judge

1st	Aunt Sudie's Funeral, Anne H. Norris, Memphis, TN
1HM	The Greening of Odie, Rebecca Davis Henderson, Cullman, AL
2HM	Right down the Middle of the Highway, Helen Thomas Allison, Memphis, TN

YOUTH AWARDS: Marcelle Nia, Judge

1st	The Waters are One, Elizabeth Young, Bountiful, UT
2nd	Headlights, Thomas H. Aldridge III, Memphis, TN
3rd	French Vanilla, Caitlin Christian Griffith, Germantown, TN
4th	A Stormy Vacation, Nathan Roberts, Searcy, AR

"Tears from a Grateful Heart," life size bronze sculpture, Artist/Sculptor: Scott Stearman, downtown, Lebanon, Ohio; photo by Laurie Boulton.

SUZUKI WARM-UPS

Pint-size Paganinis everywhere,
Sawing guilelessly away on those
Midget fiddles with half-bows as they
Perch or pretzel-sit, stand absently
About, scratching calf with foot; staring
Wide as jars, stroll off, then wander back,
Seem not aware of shaping notes nor
Any part of something larger, but
There in colonnade, here on lawn, by
Nearly any yonder, these tots' all-
Unlikely presence and their playing
Festoon the world entire. Saul Steinberg
Must have loved them; as for any Marc
Chagall, they'd float right in, and welcome.

Stephen Malin

Sun-beaded dewdrop
clings to swaying spider web
rainbow in motion

Anne-Marie Legan

WOODLAND MYSTERY

With every moon-splashed hour,
sounds quivered like restless stars.
Katydids shrieked,
whip-poor-wills mourned,
owls hooted and cried dolorously.
In the growing whisper of the wind,
the moon's mellow light
danced over rocky-caps
and down woodland paths.
Rippling lakes glistened in
watercolor coolness...
the trail, like a river of
shimmering silver,
splitting the wilderness
from earth to sky...
losing itself in the sense of
divine mystery.

Anne-Marie Legan

Sunset on Skagit Bay by David Millison

2

TO MY MOTHER

Come, take my hand. And tell me you first
Perceived the truth against which, unrehearsed,
I fought, afraid, not ever quite believing
That roles like yours and mine could be reversed
So totally. I think of you, perceiving,
And yet a willing partner in the game
I felt compelled to play. I'd call your name,
Reminding you - and me – I'd been your child
And would be always. You? You only smiled.
You were the wiser then. You knew the why, the when,
The subtleties of change, the boundaries crossed
Inevitably. It was I who lost
All battles finally.
                    Now we are at peace.
Child of your child, I watch you slowly cease
To reach beyond my hand. I understand.
And there is comfort, and a kind of growth
In this clear truth of ours. I'll keep us both.

Maureen Cannon

overcast morning
bare limbs inkblot ashen sky
cardinal appears

Michael Denington

MUSINGS OF THE MAD WIDOW

Stranger, if you come through
 the door of
Phong Fu's Chinese Restaurant
one step behind me
the waitress will mistake
us for a pair.
Join in the complicity.
Don't let your feet in dock-siders
do an embarrassed shuffle.
Wear cut-offs and surfer shirt.
I like men
who dress younger than their years.
You will know me
by my khakis and safari blouse.
Don't let me hurry to
a vacant, empty booth.
Put your body beside
across me.
Make a joyful noise. Slurp
your soup. Let the egg
drop when it will.
Getting steamed
rice together
is more fun.
Savor the piquancy of pork
waiting to be laid
in sweet-sour sauce.
Twist your way through fork-
fuls of lo mein noodles.
Then, past the conventions
of teas sipping
when we pull apart
our cookies, let the lettered
paper drop since

we've already found our fortunes
in each others lap.

Anna DeMay

BOUQUET TO THE FALLEN

Three black-barred feathers mingle in a vase
of summer's relics: grass plumes, soft and sere;
brown pods whose seeds will never swell in earth.
Mute symbols rest in doubtful glory
till a whim impelled by holidays or spring
reduces grass and pods and feathers all
to ignominy with apple peels,
the bone of Tuesday's roast, and empty cans.
Three feathers, strangely out of place and yet
half-hidden now, as in an August day
their brownness sheltered in the tall-grassed slough
from predators the bird whose tail they graced.

How futile to suggest a kiln-glazed jar
might catch the spirit of a pheasant hen.
I hope the winged one, sans three feathers, flew
to where some grass still rooted in the ground
awaits another spring and nests and young
that it may offer cover. I would not
adorn my hearth with one whose flight is done,
whose black bars count my own aborted flights.

Lucille Morgan Wilson

FOX HOLLOW

The moon calls the foxes out,
sets their blood a-racing,
but the eerie screams unsettle me.
For weeks, I search the woods,

aiming to rid the farm of the pests.
I find pawprints by the spring,
and leavings--rabbit fur and chicken
feathers, but the den's whereabouts

is a mystery. Random sightings
take me unawares: a giant fox poised
on the hilltop against the orange
sunball; a bitch in the path (she trots

away, looking back to take my measure);
a kit's pointy red face watching
from the tickseed at forest's edge.
It runs helter-skelter to the den

in the rocks by the sinkhole, where
I should've looked in the first place.
I ponder the means, but I can't bear
the pictures that arise--the feisty

rascal chewing its leg off, or riddled
with bullets, or lying stiff and bloated.
I climb the hill to the house, counting
myself blessed by the visitations.

Come twilight, I hear the screams,
like an old woman in distress,

but I am at peace, for they are friends
calling in the only language they know.

Elizabeth Howard

FULL CIRCLE

Born beneath the stars
you, my copper skin beauty
hold morning-sun-fire in your eyes.
With you snug in cradleboard laced upon my back
I climb the mountain top
to see where we must go
You open one eye to see where you have been.

I shield you in my shadow for many summers
little son
until you take flight and soar with eagles.

And now, I am old.
In winter's chill, the owl calls my name.
You lace me upon the travoise
and climb high places
to see where we must go.
I open one eye to see where I have been.

Rita Goodgame

THE BARKING

The house and I have curled ourselves
      to sleep, but the barking of a dog
         bites into my dream
    and nips at my remembering...
I am transposed to Egypt
      to the Valley of the Kings,
         to the tombs
    of Ramses and Tutankhamen,
where for centuries now deceased,
      time, wind, sand and other teeth
         have gnawed and eaten
    stories baked in stone...
where buses arrive daily
    to shake themselves free
        of cameras and tourists
    who find themselves surveyed
by hungry canines slinking about
        with tucked in tails.
Above them on a pink cliff
    a huge black mongrel tosses
bark after bark down the precipice.
      His abrasive echo bounces

      across continents
    to become my neighbor's dog.
I lie awake with the flavor
      and the grit of Egypt
    in my mouth, and I hold them
    and savor them like rawhide...

Clovita Rice

GLORY ON THE MISSISSIPPI

Far from its mighty current
And far from one idyllic afternoon,
Reflected glory riding the Mississippi
Glows in my memory's eye open yet
To imagine all I know of beauty in whatever guise—
To imagine and recapitulate that sunset-reality.

Awe-struck where I stood,
I watched the broad expanse of the river turn to blood
Then brighten to a golden spread which bore a single log
Black on the sparkling water,
Bore it through boiling, tumbling rings many-tinted
        as spilled opals;
Bore it into a smoother brightness
And past graceful circles radiating leftward
Toward the densely wooded shore,
Where a somber shadow fell on the water's ruddy flush.

In that moment, tall above the forest wall,
A clean-stemmed sycamore tree, spectral white in
        deadness,
Was struck by unobstructed splendor streaming from the
        sun,
And it waved a single bough
Glowing like flame against the changing sky.
My heart caught high as if pierced by a dazzling lance
To hold the brightness:
Pierced to stand transfixed by that reflected glory,
That transcendent beauty,
And transfused by rising joy which lasted into night.

But now, that epiphany on the river bank,
That remembered iridescence moving on the Mississippi,
Is a sad reminder of the hidden streams
That bear us all at random down the dark of life.

But I would cheat despair and darkness,
Dare to find radiant magnificence,
And have my own night remembered
As a star...burning, glowing.

Winifred Hamrick Farrar

Mississippi Poetry Journal Award, 1995

the turtle
in the grass
almost blends in

Brett Taylor

A dense fog
clouds the forest path
obscuring deer

Brett Taylor

Tiny yellow finch
swaying on a slender stalk
crunching flower seeds

Frances Darby

THE FIRE BIRDS

In the days when Pele
lived in the caldera atop Mount Waialeale,
the wind goddess blew weary finches
across two thousand miles of raging ocean
to the emerald shores of Hawaii.
Over the centuries they became birds of fire.
With feathers like the yellow in a torch flame,
 the O'o bore plumage worn by royalty.
The I'iwi, red as lava flow,
ignited the forest as it sucked
nectar from lobelia flowers.
But man came with his pigs, his ship rats
and his diseases.
Today, with only thirty species left
and half of the rest endangered,
we have become tenders of the flame,
charged with keeping Hawaiian forests
kindled with avian fire.

Mr. Russell Strauss

White, gauzy cloud-puffs
swirl by - lie - superimposed
on powder blue sky

LaVonne Schoneman

ROOF OF FLOWERS
(A Beymorlin Sonnet)

When Flo, my closest friend, had lost her mate,
I tried to comfort her, I held her hand
and, though I questioned why and doubted fate,
I cried with her and said, "I understand."

I could not understand the loss she felt,
the grabbing pain of lonely misery;
nor would I understand until death dealt
that stabbing monumental grief to me.

The wreath of death, which no one can ignore,
encased my love in bronze that plunged six feet
beneath a roof of flowers without a door.
I faced first-hand, existence incomplete.

Today Jo said, "I understand—I know"
the way I could not say it long ago.

Verna Lee Hinegardner

SOME THINGS IN LIFE

have been hard—childbirth comes to mind—
closing my father's eyes for that last long sleep,
having to make love when I felt only hate,
but the hardest was when my child,
lying gray against hospital-white sheets,
asked me to sing.

Marcia Camp

12

OBEDIENCE

Our neighbor was eager to sample
the peaches
his mail-order tree was bearing;
but before the fruit could ripen,
it was fast disappearing.

Earlier a dozen Elbertas
were shining on the tree;
but these freestones
had dwindled down now
to only a meager three.

The owner, suspecting his sons
of being the "Houdinis"
vanishing the fruit,
issued this decree:
"Whoever pulls these last three peaches
can expect a thrashing from me."

Hoping to avoid punishment, the boys made a pact
to which they agreed: they would never,
never,
never
pull those peaches from the tree

A few days later, our neighbor
was startled in his orchard
at the oddity he did see:
three naked peach seeds
clinging
defiantly
to his mail-order tree.

Lucile R. Ray

A WORLD APART

"Be careful going home," he called to me.
I did not know that this would be goodbye;
And yet before the dawn, I came to see
One-half of me give up the fight and die.

He fought that fight as men of courage do
Before his spirit flung the portals wide
And let the light of God come shining through
To smile upon his face the day he died.

In retrospect, I find him in my bone,
Like marrow from a transplant long ago
That towers over death and over stone
To live again in last year's afterglow

I keep these tongues of silence in my heart
Where yesterday I found a world apart.

Frieda Dorris, Memphis, TN

inspection reveals
crape myrtle blossoms instead
of July snowfall

Sandra O. Hancock

14

POT HOLDERS

Miniature Dutch children with turned-up caps
and crisscrossing hands clasped behind their backs
skated past windmills on delftware plates
lining the pin-neat hutch of
my knitting teacher.

She was an old woman from Holland
when we were ten-year-old girls sitting
on her living room floor each Wednesday
after school with size eight needles
and Red Heart yarn.
Dutch girls and boys, she said (rolling her 'r's),
were allowed to attend school only after
they could knit their own socks.

We knitted pot holders.

Some of us spent a whole year
on one lopsided knotted tangled square.
Lost stitches, dubbed 'buttonholes,'
were dangerous debaucheries in pot holders.
Those, we re-knit. Dutch children's
feet would freeze in socks full of buttonholes.

Some of us caught on rapidly, graduating
to house slippers with pom-pom toes.
Nancy got so good that she knit herself a pink
cardigan sweater with legitimate buttonholes.
Her reward was a tiny pair of porcelain Dutch shoes
strewn with blue and white tulips which
—I fancied—
would have looked smarter in my blue bedroom
than in her pink one.

Giggling at my knitting teacher's chortled stories,
however, I persevered with pot holders—
Christmas gifts for my mother, grandmothers,
sisters, aunts, fifth grade teacher, and knitting teacher
        (although she didn't really need one),
until my edges were keen and
each row of stitches lined up like
dutiful Dutch children in hand-knit socks.

I still watch for buttonholes when knitting a poem.

Jane Randall

AWAKENING

While
the world's
still sleeping
through the window
like a soft whisper
a song only for me
through the blinds I can see him
a small rose-breasted house finch perched
as I watch as he shyly approaches
he blinks and in small hops repeats the song
as if to say, peace, he is in God's hands now.

Louise Stoval Hays

SCENT OF CITRUS

The black silk kimono with its white embroidered
Chinese symbols still lay across the chair
where she'd tossed it— the citrus scent she favored
faintly discernable weeks after she was gone,
allowed him to pretend, for brief moments,
that his life had not ended when hers did.

Marilyn Stacy

"Every path has its puddle "
-English proverb

A puddle in the path.
A grin of splash-splattered socks.
A hawk-browed frown.
Over. No. *Around* No.
I jump! Oh joy
of brown explosion.

Laura Black

white teapot
filled with tea
roses

Frances W. Muir

17

ULTRA SOUNDS

for Mark and Shanie

The sound of my granddaughter
is soft on shining paper,
metal gray shavings like a face,
like eyes, yes I see eyes,
the sound of eyes coming at me.
She lifts arm to forehead
with a sound like waving,
like a first wave. I think
that's her forehead. Isn't
that my nose? She is too
new riding earthward on a
sound in that pink cradle.

I remember her father, a curving
fetus in my own young womb
thirty years ago in Germany.
I remember the tickle of his hands
long before pictures of sounds of hands
were ever possible. I saw him
once in a dream, his pre-formed
hands entered my mind on a silver sound
one 3:00 AM when I couldn't sleep.
A gift without paper, his eyes
moved through night sounds
to stare at me, his body still
on the other side of being.

Laminate, my daughter-in-law says.
I want to keep this picture forever.
So we put it through, cook it in plastic
and out it comes, all black and indistinct
from the heat. Some ultra sounds
can't be contained. The heat

of too much knowing
and holding on . . . burns everything.

Margo LaGattuta

SKY TRAILS

No one knows where the wild goose goes,
Nor the seagull high in the sky.
He follows a path we cannot see
Answers a call we cannot hear,
And yet he flies home with unerring grace
On a road that leaves not a trace.

Tana Harwood Ford

THE ENDLESS BEACH

In my stretched forth open hands—
Palms upturned and full of glittering sand—
I hold what was
What is and
What will be
And not a grain spills

Lois Batchelor Howard

BRAIN DANCING

Swelling and contracting with each breath
and pulsating in time to the beating heart,
the healthy brain dances within the skull.
Dr. Frank Vertosick, Jr., *Discover Magazine*

The half-moon hangs above eastern mountains,
a bowl of light, spilling by moonset
across western hills. I remember,
with each breath, thousands of nights
shared with its changing face.
Where have those sunsets gone,
passing like autumn's golden hearts
hung on the redbud tree?
What green air has swallowed
the sunrises, first light sliding over the ground,
each one new as never?
I catch glimpses of yesterday slipping
into spring, those yearning moments
hurrying down winter.
Speechless before beauty pouring
across the blue glass of tomorrow like rain,
I pile bricks of memory on the sidewalk
of time, calling down cold sunlight
to grip the forgotten until I can touch it.

I see them all—the sea, an indigo whisper
in my blood; the swaying sunflowers,
those prayers for birds, painted
on the back of my eyes;
the milkweed pods burst by summer,
their silkiness memorized by my fingertips.
They are all hidden on the shelves
of quiet neurons, waiting to be lifted
and turned like crystals to the light.

I think of them, a mere hiccup
in the memory of the moon,
and wonder at my thoughts
passed around like bowls of words.

Rosalyn Ostler

THE RHYTHM OF HER DAYS

With her black dress clinging to her legs,
she hung the wash upon the line.
It was important to go on with the routine
of her days—wash on Monday, meat loaf
on Tuesday, buy groceries on Wednesday,
that was double coupon day.
Clean her house on Thursday and visit
the sick on Friday.
John was dead now. Sitting, praying
and talking would not bring him back.
The rhythm of her days was all she had
and prayers would wait for Sunday church.
John always helped her hang the sheets,
he was here now.
Her hands needed to work, and tears
would come later when she had the time.

Betty Heidelberger

SET FREE IN INCREMENTS

I stand at the screen door
watch my husband drag out the rowboat
the old, ripped, life jacket, the one rotten oar
and I gag on my worry
will hold it there all day

he has set the borders of the jigsaw puzzle
leaving the rest for me to fill in
but I tip over the card table, will not finish his puzzle

there will be enough time later
for whatever is left of whoever survives
to complete the final picture

I walk my backyard hill that overgrows
with wild fuchsia, blackberry creepers
dense snarls of our lives, jeweled insects
that sing in syllables, forecast how, in the end
one of us will bury the other

the mature tree I once wrapped as a sapling
in burlap and chicken wire, has lost its leaves
it trembles its age through its trunk, scratches
with its stripped branches on hoary clouds
black runes that translate how
there is no quick way to loosen the tie between us
it must be set free in increments

a voice calls my name, he waves from the boat
laughs, holds up a fish, I actually see
in the sheen of the lake
the shine of my own relief, feel a sharp thrill

the entire moment becomes silver lit
astonishingly alive, silhouetted
against a darkening, navy-blue sky

then released.

Eileen Malone

THE MORNING AFTER

*I put a piece of paper under my pillow, and when I could
not sleep, I wrote in the dark.*--Henry David Thoreau

But I could not read my writing
in the morning
So I got up the next night

And light empowered
while perched on the privy

I composed on toilet paper
a perfect poem

An easy and legible elucidation
to appease the midnight muse

Until my husband in the morning
picked up my masterpiece from the floor
and flushed it down the fixture

Ellaraine Lockie

GROWING OLDER

Growing older means you may forget
Whether you brushed your teeth today--
Checking the brush to see if it's wet.

You want bacon, but eat prunes instead.
You rise slowly from sitting or bending,
Or you may become dizzy in the head.

The newspaper print has grown to small!!
You breathe hard and hold rails to climb
Flights of low stairs that now loom tall.

"Age has many blessings" may be true;
but with aching joints and failing sight
you may have trouble naming a few...

Helen Thomas Allison

A slim cat watching
Fat robins "worming" their way
Across the green lawn.

Helen Thomas Allison

Dropped from brown branches
Pinecones dot a woodland trail
Mahogany gems.

Angela Logsdon

SKIPPING STARS

One cloudless night, we made the backyard our bed,
rocky soil and tufted grass our somewhat lumpy mattress.
We shared the soft cover of darkness with mildly curious
cows
and hungry mosquitoes, while spring peepers sang their
tenor hymns
and the stars glittered, sparkling sequins on God's midnight
blue robe.

Not with the frenetic pace of fireworks,
but with an otherworldly grace and dignity,
a piece of heaven streamed from north to south.
God's glowing rock danced on our rippling atmosphere,
splitting in half, two traveling in tandem. Then,
wondrously,
one fractured again, the three leaving luminous trails
that remained long minutes to commemorate their passing.

I've heard storms shout, "I AM!" announcing God's power
as lightning ruptured the night and rain battered our
windows.
I've reveled in the frozen, feathery kisses of a silent
snowfall.
But I feel closest to God while lying in the transparent
darkness,
my Father skipping stars across our little oxygen pond
As I watch in awe.

Rhonda Roberts

Photo by Jane Allen

THE BRIDGE TO YESTERDAY
(A July Morning)

Once a thriving bridge for wagons,
buggies, bicycles,
and newly-bought cars...
        and
barefooted boys clinging to the "banister"
    with curled-down toes,
        lest they might fall
            into the *misty vapors*
                of the Conecuh River.
Now a cracked remnant of parched
concrete wrapped in kudzu vines
and tangled weeds...
        and
barefooted boys clinging to the "banister"

26

with curled-down toes,
　　lest they might fall
　　　　into the *murky cobwebs*
　　　　　　of the Conecuh River.

Jane E. Allen

Preying spider writes—
spinning stories for victims
on cobweb tablet.

Jane E. Allen

COUNTY PICKUP

You came like a thief in the night
Silent and quick, you took her
Leaving her death shroud hanging
haphazardly on her house
You left your calling card
One dog
Ten dollars, please.

Angela Logsdon

Drawing by Lenna Frye

Cold frost froze flowers
she chose for her wedding day.
She just bought imports.

Ruth Wittenberg

River iced over
One inch of fragility
floats defiant deer

Ellaraine Lockie

HOMELESSNESS

No where to go
No one to see
Nothing to do
Nothing to be
Every possession
Just a cart sleeping free.

Laurie Boulton

Photo by Laurie Boulton

MEMORIES OF A DIVORCE,
TO A NOVICE

I remember picking at the plaid cushion,
following the shadow of fern on the wall.
I heard the news, then left the room.
We were fourteen, thirteen,
Eleven and eight—
little, and dirty—puppies really.
And life goes on.
I have a red simmering,
seldom-stirred smoldering.
I am cold and hard and trying
to keep that barely bubbling still.
We heard the news, then left the room,
back to where we'd been—
my hair curlers and telephone,
my sister trotted over next door.
One brother turned on the TV,
the other went off to dig worms.
"Well, that's that. Let them go."
And we never came back
to look at the gap, the gasp, the gaping,
the momentary vacuum, the maw,
our split second chasmic free fall.
No ambulance came for our hearts.
If only I'd been a little older
I might have said something
or taken one or the other of them in my arms,
the way I hold you now.
You will probably always remember the chair
you were in, and the room.

Laura Black

SHOOTING OWLS

What is it I want to remember?
The day I shot the owl? I suppose.
Not so much that I want to remember
as that I can't forget.

It was a cottonwood, close to leafless,
and he, a silhouette against gray clouds,
ripe for picking.
Why is it every small-town boy owns a .22,
a natural extension to his arm?

I thought it all a thrill back then:
dull thud of the bullet, the feather-burst. . .
I owned the landscape, the wildlife—
I owned it all.

He ricocheted off branches as he fell.

N. Colwell Snell

POTPOURRI

Potpourri is the fragrance
Of love and life, bound with strife,
Which sweetens the closet
Of our memory.

Bettye Cannizzo

RUBBER BAND HOURS

We take Highway B
to the Meadowood Nursing Home
where Aunt Marie waits for us.
Her wrinkled hands knit and purl,
count the stitches—one by one—
as she listens for our footsteps.

At the entrance geraniums fill ceramic pots.
Here no one picks the dried flowers
clinging to life on straw-like threads.
The residents look out
through rain-spattered windows
at the brittle, balding heads...
wish to snip and prune
but— they must have permission.

These watchful eyes stare
from behind closed curtains,
envy the ivy climbing the aging brick
free to wander as it pleases.

The receptionist smiles behind black-rimmed glasses.
She points to the lounge where Aunt Marie
sits in a walnut rocking chair,
absorbed with the glassed-in birds that sing
from the branches of an artificial tree.

We glance at the others,
weathered husks that rock
to the tempo of the chirping birds.
Each chair moves with a defining squeak.
The chorus of walnut, oak, and pine
sounds like an orchestra tuning up

before the curtain is raised.
One rocker drowns out the others.
Forward. Backward. Pause.
Then, the routine begins again.

We leave this menagerie—
this respite from rubber band hours,
knowing that in one's zeal to hang this mirror,
the tenants, like the birds, have lost the brilliance
of their song.

Arla M. Clemons

A LABOR OF LOVE

A piece of wood on the shelf is a lifeless object
but the woodcarver sees something more—
a murmur, a beating pulse in the rings of tupelo.

The carver touches the block, feels the heartbeat
of the bayou shore where it all began. He muses over
this evolution within his grasp.

He sits at his bench, chisel in hand,
as an idea begins to grow.
Then he makes the first cut—
the wood chips begin to fall.

He feels the comfort of the knife in his palm.
Adrenaline rushes as the bird takes form.
Slowly, his steady hands turn and mold
as he cradles the tupelo in his callused hand.
Challenged, the carver gives uncertainty direction

as he shapes body, tail feathers, and the slender beak.
Too bulky here; he shaves away more wood.
Then, his lips tighten as his eyes
study the wingspan.

With the wood burner, the carver details
the wings, the breast, the back.
The clock moves hour by hour,
the carver losing all sense of time.

The final touch is added with the brush.
Violet blue flows until the indigo bunting evolves.
Following the bird's contour, the brush dips, strokes,
and glides as if an unseen presence
guides it.

The man lifts the bird to the light,
sighing with satisfaction.
He puts the bunting on the shelf,
quietly says, "It is finished,"
then turns off the light.

Arla M. Clemons

Whirling wind blindness,
rain, dust: dark, choking vortex,
Hurricane Ivan.

Roadside bog—stalking
White egret on dark water
splash fishing - a bream.

Thomas McDaniel

ALABAMA SPRING

Barges buoyed on the bay
A petite yellow feathered bird
Perched on a great chunk of red rock
Bobbing to banjo music.

Fragments of magnolia and cotton-like snow in
August everywhere
Southern sweet scent pine fills the air

A warm Spring fog rises
Veil of white brushed by misty wind
Dancing in the sun
Quiet as a butterfly
Landing on a dream.

Vincent J. Tomeo

JEWELS

Rain beads sparkle on a summer rose
Like the fangs of crystal that winter froze,
And the dew-pearled wheel of a spider's web,
And the dancing diamonds on the riverbed,
And the ol' sapphires of the midnight sky,
And the emerald eyes of the dragonfly.
Gold has its value, but there is more worth
In the jewels of our lovely, Grandmother Earth.

Stacy Smith

JANUARY HIGHS

Northern boys had so much on us who lived in
Southern climes—
not just Firestone Tire and Carnegie Steel,
but the free product of winter snow.

Appearance of small white flurries on still January days
aroused quiet hopes and soft dreams;
thick flakes swirling downward
like goose-filled pillows split in early morning brawls
brought sheer over-due joy.

The din of rubber feet sloshing in frigid mess
and bubbling spirits raised high to plaster walls made
for near chaos and little learning.
School would dismiss early for fear of snow-slick
roads spinning buses into deep ditches.
The one p.m. bell would send town boys running,
sliding, cavorting in and round,

even the most reluctant daring a ball or two today.

But the real object was the hill.
There mid left-over fall mock oranges half rotted on
          late autumn green,
boys trudged slowly up the high old hill
lined with leafless Bois d' Arc trees
staring down like sleepy soldiers daring to be roused.

Successful ones who reached the top
stepped on brown cardboard sleds with cautious
          touch.
They pressed slowly against the white crystals
          underneath,
a crunchy sound echoing from sled to sled

rumbling through the sleepy hollow below.
Then with quick, short push from the rear
the sleds spurted down the snow-covered ground
giving new life to thrill-hungry youth,
as we held heads high against the cold breeze cutting
away at Southern noses
unaccustomed to icy bursts of Northern wind.

The cost of slight frost bite was worth it all.
Once each year we all reach new highs
even in low valleys where bare trees are not wont
        to sing.

            John W. Crawford

WOLVES OF WINTER

A north wind,
cold and wet as a puppy's nose,
startles the delphiniums,
kisses the soft skin
of late blooming roses.
It hop scotches up
the bare limbs of late November,
rattles twigs, a sound of dry bones.
It kicks up the dust of summer,
sweeps it into memory,
then howls past the moon,
brings the wolves of winter
snapping at its heels.

        Charlene Villella

POETICALLY SPEAKING

I make no claims
as to being a poet;
blank verse draws a blank;
couplets, sestets and tercets
are 'ets that I don't get.

So as to the bliss
of word play ploys
and rhyming joys,
inclusive the other 'ets
o'er above mentioned
and not my lot to get,
I will eat poetic humble pie.
Admit to being talent shy.

With no pentameter heroic,
or otherwise,
coming in ten drum beats
to sweep me off my size ten feet,
albeit not knowingly iambic,
I will depart the poetry game
and write a best seller instead.

Cornelius Hogenbirk

Waterfall

Crystal liquid
    free f
        a
        l
          l
       s
    down
  as Mother Nature
       bejewels
    one of her many f
             l
               o
                w
              i
            n
          g
        gowns
          into a
      tranquil pool
    and mesmerizes
    a solitary beholder
      in awe of the
  enchanting spectacle

Stacy Smith

rambling pink roses
in old church cemeteries—
dusty country roads

Faye Williams Jones

AS BREATHS DRAW INWARD

The match cracks incandescent,
its signature crawling

in the silence of brush.
So the forest entraps its own
and eyes go mad
as all things wood-caged
clatter with the energy of fear.

Lenses flash. On retinas
each blaze reveals its duplicate,
while twigs explode in fireballs
like the staccato of bullets
discharging numerously, echo upon echo.
Within the flowerbursts of flames
animals careen, their eyes
pasting their shapes, their luminous tissues
upon the withering of green.

Now the hills are the Devil's furnace,
violent with smoke and fire...
the stench of burning.
Trees fall endlessly.
There is a vanishing of air
as breaths draw inward to no space
and *eyes* evaporate.

Isabel Joshlin Glaser

A MORATORIUM: NO MORE NATURE POEMS? NO MORE NATURE!

A lazy afternoon beside the river;
fourteen of us gather to read poetry.
An oil painting kind of day, while puffy
clouds drift slowly in a Madonna-blue
sky and on a bleached cypress stump a male limpkin
stretches his neck and preens
his wing feathers; then skims above the still
water, screaming, dripping low to create
little splashes as he performs nature's
poem, against a backdrop of far shoreline
and soaring egrets. A few bumps rise in
the water—just a quick sight of the gray,
cow-snouted face of a young manatee.
The natural river sounds are destroyed
by the loud whirring of a motor boat.

We returned to our poetry but peace
is shattered as one by one motor boats
course up and down the river forcing us
to shout our words, ruining the poem's
rhythm and no longer can we ignore
the opposite shoreline. Once birds
and wild animals lived in the shelter
of trees and bushes; where condominiums
now bloom. With them came many motor boats
to bring a violence to our river.
No longer can we read our poems. Instead
we turn our concern to the manatee;
a gentle gray mammal, too clumsy—too
slow—to avoid the sharp propellers.

We cry, "save the manatees" but mankind
has firmly set a course of destruction:
condominium barriers—and boats
always more powerful, ever faster—
and . . . death to the river's natural life.

41

The fourteen of us mourn for our river.
Once more the limpkin screams.
But who is listening?

Madelyn Eastlund

I, THE MOUNTAIN

Trees grow up my slopes
And I hear birds sing and nest
In branches that tent over
The wild animals that
Crouch, crawl, leap,
Amble, run, or dig upon me.
The rain pummels or
Washes me in gentle showers and
Turns my clay sod to a deeper rust,
Clouds and light patterning my attire
In raiment ever changing
As stones and rocks roll from my shoulders and
Stop abruptly at my feet. . .
And sometimes I feel so old and cold,
My white hair crusting and

Flaking on my balding head.
But then the sun comes...months of sun...
I feel young again!
I hear God's music everywhere;
Angels are dancing at my temple, and
I can see all around...
Why, yellow buttercups
Are growing between my toes.

Lois Batchelor Howard

DESERT NIGHT DRIFTING

This blue moon
has forsaken us
behind a bank of clouds
leaving our desert a pale sea
of tranquility against night.
Flat shadows lie
belly up under each plant
whose roots grip frozen ground.
Silence is deep as obsidian ocean
where gray whales
nose newborns to surface
then echo sonorous life-songs
that bloom and ride tides
to shoreline. Stones absorb vibrations,
ripple a thousand miles inland.
Perched at the window
my moon-eyed cat quivers,
purrs in shadowed reflections,
then delicately licks pane
drinking our breath from liquid night.

Kolette Montague

A whisper...
The rumor has started
It flows and grows
Taking on a life of its own
Until
The truth comes out
Childbirth

Nancy Watts

JOSEPH SPEAKS

I was there when he was born.
We were battered by the hostile cold until
I helped her into the squalid stable.
It smelled of dung,
but we breathed the warmth of animals.
Her pains seared closer and closer
as she scratched the straw from a manger,
refilled it with fresh then
tore a swatch from her undergarment.
I laid my cloak inside out
upon the littered dirt floor,
gentled her onto it,
tended her,
accepted her offering,
separated them,
cleaned him with a kerchief,
and placed him in her arms.
She eased him to her breast.
I watched him suckle,
knowing who he was.
But, you are my son also, I thought,
as I opened the door to the world.

Patricia W. Smith

Home is
not just a house
nor memories long past
but home is family and friends
and love.

Frances Darby

VIEW FROM A MISSISSIPPI RIVER COTTON SACK

She was one of the children who walked the cotton
patch from spring until fall stooped
with a sharp blade segregating weeds
from cotton stalks from sunrise until sundown
until the summer was almost gone...
praying for shade—daring to hope for rain.
In September she came home from school
to harvest the white gold that stole Saturday leisure
and made her curl up inside herself
like the soft balls wanting release from dark claws.
Unlike the children of the sharecroppers
she could escape to school
while they slaved on until the tyrant crop was gone.
Her parents loved her but they too had been
children of the poor and didn't know any other way.
She was slower than the rest;
she would pick enough cotton to make a bed
then lie down hidden within the foliage
and find pleasure in the sound of dry leaves crushing
and in releasing the soft white fiber
like pulling dreams from cotton candy.
Younger Bobby and Janice always weighed in more
when it was time to go...
during the ride home nestled in soft cotton piled high
with the warm smell of harvested clouds,
she gave in to the magic and
forgave dark claws.

Frances Brinkley Cowden

Reprinted from the collection,
View from a Mississippi River Cotton Sack
published by Grandmother Earth,1993 and 1994.

Cover of *The Walking Stick* Literary Magazine by
Patrick Banks

YOUNG AUTHORS and ARTISTS

THE WATERS ARE ONE

Perhaps
when the Atlantic
and Mediterranean
meet
they whisper of ships
lost on icy nights,
how it is to lap against
East Coast big-city steel,
of Italian cities-to flow
through carrying
tourist-carting gondolas,
and some news
from the Nile.
Perchance,
when the Yellow River
sloshes into the Pacific,
they chatter near the rocks
about irrigating fields
harvested by people
in pointed hats,
of glimpses of travelers
walking the Great Wall,
of luaus on
the Hawaiian Islands,
and L.A. smog.
And do the rivers
of Western Europe—
the land I most wish
to visit—gossip
about a silly, young

brown-haired girl who
while visiting Missouri
leaned near the bow
of a Mississippi steamboat,
and pretended to be
on the Titanic?

Elizabeth Young, Grade 9

MY VIEW OF THE GREAT DEPRESSION

based on the book, *Naked Ears*, by Altha Murphy

We didn't have very much
with the Great Depression going on and such.
But we made do with what we had.
and we never were too sad.
We didn't have fancy toys
to cherish and enjoy.
But we did have homemade dolls
and the boys would play ball.
We entertained ourselves just fine
usually, when playing games we ran out of time.
Our meals were pretty predictable,
but we always had something to eat.
and sometimes when a little extra money happened
our way, we got a special treat.
A favorite of mine was bologna and
store-bought light bread—
we always ate so much of it, you'd think
we were never fed.

Whitney Brinkley, Grade 9

HEADLIGHTS

Life is approaching headlights.
It appears dim,
In the distance at first glimpse.
It grows in brightness,
Lessens in distance,
And comes much faster than
You'd really like to admit.
Then, when it's right up on you,
And you think you can make it out,
The glare hinders your vision,
And it passes quicker than it was found.
Death is passing headlights.

Thomas H. Aldridge III, Grade 12

RAINBOW ROW

Rainbow Row isn't just a street
He is a cat you'd love to meet
His color is gray, but they call it blue
It just doesn't mean that he is sad too
He loves to pounce and have some fun
He is really fast, and loves to run
He drinks from the toilet bowl, plays with the fish,
And stalks the hamster against our wish
He is furry, but not fat
Rainbow is our Maine Coon cat

Courtney Watts, Grade 7

FRENCH VANILLA

I like French vanilla.
So did Grandma. She smelled like it,
    and Grandpa smelled like tobacco.
And Aunt Rose smelled like a toad.
And Uncle Jim smelled like the fin
    of a blue trout, because he fished all day.
When he was out, Grandma
    would make cookies and tea.
And when I was little I'd say: "All for me?"
And she would laugh and we'd play patty cake.
And I'd jump rope and she'd drink Coke.
But now she's gone.
I don't know if I can go on, because my heart
    feels so empty without Grandma.
And her French vanilla scent.

Caitlin Christine Griffith, Grade 9

ALL ABOUT ME

My hair is the color of uneaten chocolate
My bones are like long sticks
My feet are as smelly as a mule's and
My head is as big as a computer
But my heart holds a smile
That is as big as the sun

Christopher Watts, Grade 5

A STORMY VACATION

Nathan Roberts, Grade 6

Pitter   pat!   Pitterpatter....Pitter-patter
pitterpitterpitter   patter   patter   patapataPATTER-
PATTERPATTER! The shower steadily grows
stronger, drenching everything in its path as it blows
across the landscape.

I have many memories of the past, but one
particular memory that I like to think about is of a
vacation we took on the coast of North Carolina.

Rain bounced off of the roof of our private
beach house, just like it is now. All of a sudden, ---
ZZAAP! All the power in our beach house went
kaput. "Shoot!" I exclaimed, staring at the blank
screen of our Super Cinema Wide Screen TV. I saw
distant clouds outside. Bewildered, I continued to look
out over the ocean and into the drizzly, overcast sky.
Little did I know that the small shower would soon
grow to become a relentless destroyer. . .

The winds slammed against our little beach
home. The radio announced that a small tropical storm
in the Atlantic had grown into a hurricane. It had not
been named. It was now off the coast of South
Carolina. It was moving northwest.

We immediately gathered food, a flashlight,
and the radio and rushed into the storm cellar. We
heard a rumble and a crash. Then, the storm cellar
jerked and we all bashed into the wall. No one was
seriously hurt, though.

A couple of hours later, the radio announced
that Hurricane Lina, as it was named, had shrunk and
disintegrated. We got out of the storm cellar only to

find half of the kitchen wall missing. Other than that, minimal damage was done.

I like to think about that memory and try to answer the question, "Why didn't the plates fly off into someone else's roof?" Maybe you have memories like that, too. Listen to the sounds of nature and maybe you will recall a memory or two, whether it's about a natural disaster, or just the "pitterpatter"ing of rain on the window.

***

Drawing by Courtney Cole, Grade 12

WHAT GOES AROUND COMES AROUND

Reza Alexander Zarshenas, Grade 9

One bright day in the summer of 1999, Reza was walking through the park. Reza was a short boy with hardly any muscles and was around 12 years old. He had black hair brown eyes and slightly tanned skin. He was looking for his friend, Tim. As he strolled he saw some kids he recognized. They were Thomas, Jonathan, Billy, and four other kids.

Thomas was the leader of his group. He was a little bit bigger than your average kid. He was about 13 years old with short hair, brown eyes and brown hair. Jonathan was the muscle of the group. He was a huge 15-year-old kid with short black hair and brown eyes. Jonathan wasn't a fast runner, but he was not all fat since he had a good portion of muscle. A few punches from him would make any kid cry or knock him out. He had hardly any intelligence; he failed the third grade twice. Billy is about 14 years old and is the brains of the group. He wasn't book smart but he was street smart. He was also a good fighter. He knew almost all of the pressure points in your body. He could beat up kids bigger than him and put anyone in an arm lock that would give great pain to his victims. Although, he isn't a big kid, in fact he is skinny, he makes up for his size with his skills.

Reza hated these guys because they often picked on him by making fun of his name or race. He wished he could beat them up, but he knew he couldn't. They outnumbered and outmatched him. So, Reza, with an angry expression, looked straight ahead to find Tim.

But Thomas, having nothing better to do, called out, "Hey, Raisin Bran!" Reza immediately reacted by turning around and giving him a hard look. Reza was very sensitive about the pronunciation of his name. By making fun of his name, Thomas was pushing all of his buttons. "Raisin Bran, want to come over here and have some Reese's Pieces?" asked Thomas.

Reza's face grew red and he answered, "You had better stop it, I'm warning you!"

Thomas and his group started to giggle and chanted, "Raza, Raza, Raisin, Reeza, Reese's Pieces."

Then Thomas walked up to Reza and challenged, "What are you going to do about it, Raza?"

At this point Reza had all that he could take. So Reza pushed Thomas and punched him in the face in rage. But Thomas wasn't really hurt by this punch. He instantly punched Reza in the stomach knocking the wind out of him. Then Jonathan punched Reza in his face and knocked him to the ground. Reza stayed there for five seconds before he could catch his breath and get up. There was a blood on his lip and tears on his eyes. Not all of these tears were tears of pain; they were tears of rage, hate and anger.

Reza charged forward and yelled out as he began to throw punches at Thomas and Jonathan. After the first ten, Reza began to tire. And when he began to tire, Billy got Reza in an arm lock. Reza struggled to get out but it seemed to be useless. Thomas was quite satisfied when he started to punch Reza while they held him down. Reza was like a punching bag. He was punched and kicked. They even hit him with low blows once or twice. Reza was exhausted and in pain from the beating.

Then, all of a sudden, a tall slightly muscular boy with short black hair and brown eyes came out and punched one of the boys that Reza didn't know right in the gut, followed by an uppercut. While attention was on the boy, Reza broke free, jumped up and kicked Thomas in his chest and turned around and attacked Billy. But Billy put Reza in another arm lock

Then Jonathan tackled the boy by surprise from behind. "Thanks for helping me out Tim. You did your best," said Reza.

"Well I would have done a better job if someone hadn't cheap shot me in the back like a little sissy," said Tim in a smart-alecky way.

Thomas got up and started to smile as he said, "Now you are going to get it."

Then, all the sudden, a boy out of nowhere cried out as he did a spinning roundhouse kick into Thomas's face and a backhand fist to Billy's head. Reza quickly got up and helped break Tim loose. Quickly, Thomas and his clique fled.

As Reza looked at the tall, skinny boy with red hair and freckles, he knew that he was his old friend Paul. After learning what had happened, Paul asked Reza if he wanted to learn karate. Reza was determined to learn karate, so he could kick Thomas' butt. So Reza accepted the invitation to the karate class and started to go there every Monday and Thursday.

Things changed after Reza started taking the class. He didn't just learn how to fight. He learned how to do many things: controlling his anger, being more disciplined, showing respect to everyone (especially to the ones in charge), how to avoid fights if possible. He also built up his self- confidence. As for the fighting part, he learned how to throw faster, more accurate, and more powerful punches and kicks. He also learned how to block, dodge, see the move before it came by the emotions of the opponent, deflect, flip other people, and use and get out of grabs and arm locks. Most of this was practiced and/or learned by sparring.

Sparring is a sport kind of like kickboxing, except a little different. You use the same padding and gear in it. But instead of beating your opponent into a pulp you have to get three points. You can only get one per round. If you and your opponent score a point at the same time it doesn't count. You get these points by hitting your opponent in the head, chest, kidneys, and under the arms. Not only do you have to hit your opponent in those areas, the judge has to see it clearly and see you hit him first. If you hit the opponent below the belt, other than the footgear, you will get a warning. If you get more than one warning you can lose a point, which can really mess you up. Another way you could get a warning is by using unnecessary force. If you use too much force (like breaking bones, causing excessive bleeding, or severe pain) you could be disqualified. Another important thing is to stay in the ring and hold your ground. If you constantly leave the ring for any reason, you can lose a point.

Three years have passed since the day of the fight. Reza is now stronger, faster, and wiser. He even won three tournaments in sparring won a match, winning three points after getting his left arm sprained in the third round. He never really is in a fight outside of competition now because he never   chooses to, and most people don't try him as much as they used to. Now that he knows how to fight, he doesn't need to.

This summer Reza started training with weights to increase his speed. He also started to exercise at the park. While he was jogging though the park he saw something he could relate to. He saw a little boy being teased and picked on by a group of kids. The little boy was fighting the group but beaten down and then helped by another boy. Then they were later beaten down. As Reza finally fully recognized the situation he took action.

He ran toward the bullies and jumped up and did a spinning round house kick to one of the boys that happened to be kind of big with brown hair and brown eyes and did a backhand fist to a skinnier boy with blond hair and blue eyes. He quickly leaned to the side and threw four mighty roundhouse kicks to a big slightly tubby boy with short black hair. That sent the big boy down. One of the other boys immediately tried to catch Reza off guard and charged at him, throwing a dozen punches. But due to Reza's cat-like reflexes, he was able to block all the boys' punches and counter attack for every two punches the boys threw. Every attempt to beat Reza failed.

After all of the ineffective attempts, the bullies had enough beating for that day; so they got up and ran away. Reza helped the little boy up and asked if he was okay. After Reza found out what happened, he asked the boy, "Do you want to learn karate?"

***

Drawing by Christina Brooks, Grade 12

AUNT SUDIE'S FUNERAL
Anne H. Norris

Aunt Sudie's funeral service was just like her-
- "one of a kind." It was the only time anyone could
remember chairs having to be placed in the aisle for
the overflow crowd at Hooland's Mortuary, and folks
were standing along the walls as well. Both the caring
and the curious came to pay their respect for Aunt
Sudie, who had been a fixture in our town for nearly a
century. She never had married and had outlived all
her relatives. When asked why she had remained a
spinster, her reply always would be, "I never found a
suitor who suited me." That was understandable by
those of us who knew her well for we all
acknowledged that she marched to her own drummer.
She was opinionated and stubborn as a mule, yet
respected even by those who opposed many of her
questionable actions.

With no blood-kin family, Aunt Sudie
adopted our whole town. As far as she was
concerned, we were her nieces and nephews, and all
except a few newcomers referred to her as Aunt
Sudie. As long as most of us could remember, she
had lived alone in the white two-story house, passed
down to her through several generations. Her
neighbor next door mowed her yard, and the local
grocer delivered her orders. She did not hesitate to
ask for assistance when needed. If she had a roof
leak, she simply would ring up one of her
neighbor/nephews on her old dial telephone. "This is
Aunt Sudie," she would say, "and I have a problem
that I know you can handle." Usually he could and he
did, knowing his payment would be a hug and a pat
on his back.

Aunt Sudie had planned her funeral service to
the minutest detail. She had written instructions that it

was to be held on a Sunday. (Since she had passed on into Glory on a Tuesday, this delayed the service for five days.) She had explained that she knew everyone in town would want to attend her funeral, and a Sunday service would accommodate those who had to work on weekdays. Also, should her death come earlier in the week, this simply would allow more time for visitation—which has always been a time for socializing for our town.

The service, according to her instructions, should begin at 2:00 p.m. This would be convenient for those who attend the 11:00 o'clock church service by giving them time to stop at the cafeteria for lunch. She knew this would include just about everybody in town. An additional consideration was that they already would be appropriately dressed. Aunt Sudie felt overalls and other such work clothes were not suitable for funeral attendance and she had been known to loudly voice this opinion at some most inappropriate times.

Having declared me some years earlier to be her unofficial caregiver, I had my own specific instructions. "Don't let them bury me in some pink, lace-trimmed gown," she had said, "I want to be wearing that pretty red dress I got at the Methodist rummage sale." Aunt Sudie knew the dress had been donated by Darlie Smith, our mayor's wife, who had gained too much weight to wear it. That likely is the reason Aunt Sudie bought the dress. Although no one could say it was done purposely, it seemed she wore the dress anytime she knew she would be in the company of Darlie.

Aunt Sudie often was heard to say that flowers were for the living, not the dead. "But if my burial policy provides for flowers," she had said to me, "just make sure they are 'happy flowers' and not those sweet-smelling pink carnations." She wanted her casket spray to be in bright colors, in celebration of her passing on to her new home in Glory.

Although she left a few aspects of the service up to our minister, she had told him to draw it out as long as possible. "I'd like for the Jubilee Choir to sing a few numbers, but not sorrowful songs, and be sure they sing 'I'll Fly Away' at the end. A lot of the men folks probably will have to give up a ballgame to come and I think they should be rewarded with some good music for attending." She further had instructed that it would not be necessary to give specifics about her life. "After all," she said, "everyone will know me or they wouldn't be there."

I think Aunt Sudie probably was looking down upon her funeral service and was pleased to see it was well attended and went according to her instructions. Although she had said she would try to communicate with me from her new home, as yet I have not heard from her. I imagine she is still too busy adjusting her wings, greeting old friends and offering unwanted advice to Management.

Photo by Brett Taylor

WHEN THE FEVER CAME TO TOWN: MOLLY'S STORY

Sarah Hull Gurley

I set the candle on the table beside the bed, open my journal and dip my pen in the ink bottle. The pen scratches words of my story onto the paper.

Sat. July 27, 1878—Memphis—

The weather is hot and dry; the streets dusty, unlike our cabin on Wolf River. Colin left for New Orleans this morning on the Mary Belle with a load of corn. I pray the Belle gets a return load before this baby is born.

Yesterday Colin borrowed a wagon and moved the boys and me here to stay with his folks. His parents, Agnes and Domonic have always treated me like a daughter, so I shouldn't complain. They love Marten and Thomas. Agnes thinks Marten is so smart to be only five. Thomas will be three on August 15. Maybe the baby will come on his birthday. Colin says this one's a girl. . . .

I lay my pen down and close my eyes. Last night Colin held me close and rubbed my big belly like he was caressing the baby.

"A girl for sure, Molly," he said kissing me, "with your auburn hair."

"How do you know?" I teased.

"I know. We'll name her Katherine, after your ma, and call her Katie."

Tears sprang to my eyes as I remembered Ma. Although her mass of auburn curls were streaked with gray my mother was still so full of life. Until 1873. Yellow Fever. Da wouldn't accept it; barricaded himself in the house with a case of whiskey. The house caught fire, but the neighbors couldn't save him.

Colin and I'd just built our cabin on the Wolf. Marten was baby. We begged Ma and Da to come stay with us, but they thought they were safe. Now I shake my head; try to scatter the awful memories.

Monday, Aug. 5

I am sick in my heart. Domonic came home today with frightful news of dozens of cases of yellow fever. Said that people are leaving town in droves. Trains are full, people still clamoring to get on top of the cars. When the boys were asleep, we sat at the table trying to figure out what to do. Agnes told Domonic I couldn't go far because the baby had dropped and could come at any time. Anything upsetting might make it come sooner. Domonic thinks we should stay; quarantine ourselves. We're out a ways; he thinks we're safe. We have the garden, food Agnes canned, chickens for eggs and meat, and goats for milk. Domonic will fetch other supplies tomorrow. We said the Rosary and asked the Holy Mother to watch over us.

Agnes and I watch at the window for Domonic's return with the goods.

"In all my days, I don't think I've ever seen anything like this," Agnes said.

I nodded. The street's full of escaping people. Carriages and wagons own the road; scatter people on foot like chickens. An appalling sight.

"Look at that woman," Agnes said, pointing to a thin figure in a faded print dress. A baby was strapped to her bosom, an older one to her back. She was pulling a bundle tied on a wide board with a rope.

Agnes shook her head. "Running to something probably worse than she's running from. How far can she get?"

"The two babies. She's trying to save them," I said.

Agnes put her arm around me. "Don't you worry, Molly, Sophy's the best mid-wife in town. When it's time, Domonic'll ring the bell over the well and she'll be here. We'll take care of you."

I can't sleep. I pull on my dressing gown and go into the yard. The sky is lit with stars. I find Orion and feel closer to Colin. He loves the night sky and is teaching me the constellations.

"Child, what are you doing out here?"

I'm startled by Domonic's voice. "Looking at the stars."

"Well, get back in the house. You don't want to catch the fever. Sophy says it's caused by fomites traveling at night and clinging to your clothes. Come on."

I follow Domonic back into the house.

Thursday, Aug. 29 in the city . . . of the dead

My spirit is crushed and my will to live kept alive only by the hope that Colin will soon be here. I cannot sleep. The wheels of the death wagons creak all day and all night, piled high with rough plank boxes. They've run out of coffins.

Little Katie was born a week ago today and has a head full of red hair. Her brothers never saw her. Little Thomas took sick on the 13th and Marten on the 16th. For four days they shook with fever that the

calomel and other potions could not relieve.
I was distraught. Without Agnes, I couldn't have
prepared their little bodies for burial.

Domonic was next. He lasted longer. The wagon
came for him today. Agnes is beside herself with
grief. I am too numb to feel.

Wednesday, Sept. 4—

Agnes has the fever. Started with a headache
three days ago, followed by chills and fever.
Coughing up black stuff, sometimes blood. The nuns
from St. Mary's come by with tea and what they can
manage. Little Katy still alive.

Sunday Sept. 8—

Agnes is worse. Talking out of her head about
Ireland, calling for her ma. She's burning with fever
and keeps ripping her clothes off. The sisters found a
nurse for her. They confined Katie and me to my
room. Pray God we survive.

Wed. Sep. 11—

Poor Agnes passed on yesterday. Sister Margaret
had to get the constable to make the wagon pick her
up today. Sister brought me a letter from Colin she
found stuck in the fence. He was detained on
President's Island for a week. They wouldn't let him
come here; sent him on a boat to the cabin. As soon
as he can; he's coming to me, no matter what. My
spirit breathes. So does Katie. For now.

OTTO, OLIVIA AND OSCAR

THE SAGA OF THREE OCEANIC OTTERS

Betty Gifford

Once upon a time there was a family of Sea Otters who lived in the Pacific Ocean on the Southern Coast of California in the United States of America. They swam, feasted, and played at a place known on maps as Point Conception. Their habitat was in a rocky coastal area very near the land where it was protected from wind and waves. In a warm kelp bed, they would wrap the kelp around themselves sometimes to keep from drifting out to sea. The kelp also provided camouflage with its network of heavy stemlike stipes and leafy blades. The stipes and blades also helped calm and quiet the water, as well as supporting many of the organisms sea otters like to eat.

Father, Otto, Mother, Olivia and baby, Oscar, lived happily in the cold waters of the Pacific Ocean. When Oscar was very young, Mother could be seen lying on her back, surfing on the waves, while baby Oscar ate his meals, lying on her stomach and nursing. When Oscar got too big for this type of feeding, Otto and Olivia taught him how to catch all sorts of sea creatures.

Some of the food Oscar and his parents enjoyed were fish, sea urchins, crabs, and mollusks such as clams, mussels, snails, squid, octopus and abalone. A veritable feast of sea food! Otto and Olivia taught young Oscar to dive to the ocean bottom to retrieve his food. They showed him how they collected it in their paws and stuffed it under the loose skin of a forearm to carry it back to the surface. Then they would lie on their backs and break open the hard-shelled food, either by force of their paws or by constantly hitting it with a rock.

What fun they had, day and night, diving deep and swimming hard for their food, then relaxing on their backs, stuffing their stomachs. Oscar was only a few weeks old when Olivia taught him to swim. She took him to a quiet area, slipped out from underneath him and stayed just out of range, coaxing him to swim to her. He floundered a few times, and she was there to catch him; then, all of a sudden, he got the hang of it, and off he went, swimming like a pro! His first strokes were made while he lay on his belly, but he soon got the hang of floating on his back. By two or three months, he was swimming along side his mother. That's when she taught him to dive. Diving took strength and skill since the pup's coat was so buoyant. At first when he was diving, he would bring up pebbles, seaweed scraps and other useless material. It was fun, but not very filling or nourishing. Finally, Oscar caught on that they were seeking their food, and that was even more fun!

And, then, there was play time! Racing, playing leapfrog, wrestling, somersaults -- you name it, they played it! Oscar played with his mother, mostly, but sometimes other adults would join in and that was really fun!

And, then, one day, it all came to an end! Oscar had been warned of certain dangers, such as killer whales and sharks in the water. But he had also been taught how to freeze, play dead or dive for safety in a kelp bed. So those big fish weren't really that much of a danger. And he knew how to stay alert while on land

and look out for coyotes or bald eagles. No one had told him about oil, though.

One morning early, just after the big yellow globe in the sky had risen, Oscar, Olivia and Otto began their brief grooming of their fur, then dove for their food. Rising from the ocean, they drifted for several hours, enjoying the sunshine and the clams they had found. They even took a nap for a while.

When they woke up they felt very strange. Their fur was all matted up and smelled terrible! The sea around them was all yucky, filled with a scum of oily mess! They couldn't breathe very well, and, in swimming quickly for shore, swallowed some of the slimy stuff. On land, they lay there, unable to rise, gasping for breath. By the time the big yellow globe in the sky had vanished, so had the lives of Otto, Olivia and Oscar. They were found the next day by some people who had come to see the destruction manifested by the spill of the oil from the tanker.

If there were no oil tankers to spring leaks and destroy the natural habitat and the creatures that live there, Otto, Olivia and Oscar would have lived for at least fifteen or twenty years. As would all of the other creatures destroyed at that time. Otto, Olivia and Oscar were just three of the many! Farewell, little furry, lovely creatures! You brightened our planet for a brief while! Thank you!

LONG WALK HOME

Martha A. McNatt

In the distance a clock chimed midnight as two silent figures emerged from a darkened theatre, moved quickly down a deserted alley and disappeared into the night. Moments later, a military patrol unit moved into place in the theatre district, but detected no violation of the curfew now in place in the city of Hamburg, Germany. It was late May 1945, almost three weeks after the German government had surrendered to Allied forces, ending the European phase of World War II.

The two figures moved single file into a residential area of the city and walked silently along a narrow street. They were dressed in the garb of country German women, heavy shoes, long skirts and babushka-covered heads. One carried a large handbag of cheap tapestry, and the other had a duffle bag over her shoulder bulging with what appeared to be bedding. The handle of a cooking pot was visible above the knotted closing of the bag. Both women were of stocky build with slightly stooped posture. They continued their steady but unhurried path through silent streets and within an hour were near the city's southern outskirts where they stopped to rest underneath a bridge.

The appearance of the two women was deceiving. In reality they were two cousins, Freida and Marta, ages twenty-two and twenty. They had grown up in Freiburg almost three hundred miles southwest of Hamburg. Marta was a singer and Freida a pianist, who had spent the last two years working with a troupe of actors and musicians entertaining for the German military. (In the manner of the American USO.)

Freida was born into a middle class German family in the mid twenties. Music was an integral part of life in her family and her parents struggled to pay for piano lessons beginning at age seven. She was a talented student who played Chopin brilliantly but she developed a love for the bawdy drinking songs of the German country folk and the pop music played in Cabaret Lounges in Southern Germany and France. As World War II swept across Europe, Freida joined a troupe of entertainers traveling to the major cities in Germany. She soon found a place for Marta. The two cousins traveled together with the group for two years, and they were in Hamburg when the German surrender occurred. For a few days the performers continued to hang around the Opera House, not knowing what to expect when the Allied Occupation Forces arrived. Within a week Canadian troops occupied the city. The entertainers were informed that they were to be a part of a massive clean up and rebuilding program of Western Europe, which had been flattened by the war.

Both cousins were attractive young women. Freida was tall with flaming red hair and the graceful posture of a dancer. Marta was blonde, petite, and shapely. The two cousins had become very close during their two years on the road and they decided to defy the order to join the reconstruction efforts of the Allies. Confiscating clothing and boots from the theatre prop room they transformed themselves to appear as middle-aged country women. In the darkness of their tiny bedroom they decided to walk the three hundred miles from Hamburg to Freiburg by traveling on narrow country trails and back roads. Whispering in the darkness with a small flashlight under their blanket, they planned their route, marked it on a map, and memorized every road village and turn. They pooled their money and stashed it in their shoes.

By daylight they were outside the city walking along a narrow paved road heading south. Since it was late spring, they were able to forage for food along the countryside. They slept in abandoned barns and bombed out buildings. They were often able to buy sausages and bread in the villages of the Northern Plain. They could sometimes find shelter in the village churches. At other times, the environment was unfriendly and they endured hunger, thirst, and fatigue. They often saw military convoys along the roads but they managed to hide in the underbrush or to blend into the environment and were never challenged. For four months they walked. At times they could travel only a short distance in a day because of the terrain and the resulting sore and blistered feet.

In early autumn the women reached the city of Freiburg. They came to Marta's home first. Her parents were there, safe from the ravages of war but penniless and needing medical attention. After two days of rest, Freida set out for her own home fifteen miles away. When she arrived the house was crumbling but in the rubble she found a note from her parents telling her they were safe and where they had relocated. She walked another ten miles to find them. Her father had worked all summer accumulating enough wood for the oncoming winter. Her mother harvested and stored dried fruits and vegetables, but their savings were almost gone. Freida knew she needed to find a job in order for the family to survive another cold season.

She brightened her hair to its former shade of red, bought a pair of high-heeled shoes, a bottle of red nail enamel and began the rounds of prospective places of employment. Within days Freida was able to find employment in a beer garden where American airmen gathered for rest and relaxation. There she met Bobby, a soft-spoken Tennessee farm boy who fell in love with her at first sight. In spite of the language barrier they were married within a few months in the neighborhood Lutheran Church.

When he was discharged, they came home to Middle Tennessee where they raised a family. She eventually became a university professor, teaching her native language to the sons and daughters of the Americans who forever changed the course of her people in Germany.

****

Santorini, Greece by Mary E. Halliburton

THE AGES OF WOMAN

Madge Lewis

In the youth of middle age—the year was 1963—I became a travel consultant. During the early stages of my career, my duties involved traveling to Europe in the winter to make advance group bookings at hotels. European hotels could not accommodate the vast crowds of Americans who set siege to its capitals from early spring to late fall and for that reason the travel agency reserved rooms far in advance. Deregulation of the airlines had not yet taken place and the golden era of the travel industry was at its peak.

After one of these demanding assignments, I took a three day holiday in Switzerland. That year my business trip ended in Geneva two weeks before Christmas. I boarded a train to Visp, changing there to the narrow-gauge railroad that transported me higher and higher to the fairy tale village of Zermatt in the Alps.

The train came to a stop at dusk. December snow fell in big fluffy flakes. An enterprising Swiss lad had set up a stall near the station and the smell of bratwurst sizzling on his grill filled the air. The skiers, coming in from their day's activity, crowded around him, unable to bypass the tantalizing aroma.

The traditional policy of the village permitted no motor-driven vehicles within town limits, thus creating an atmosphere quite different from the streets of other cities. I was transferred by a sleigh pulled by a prancing horse, his nostrils flaring, breathing smoke into the cold air, the bells on his harness jingling a merry tune.

After the coachman loaded my luggage, we started down the narrow street which is the heart and soul of Zermatt. Hotels and elegant shops lined both sides, and in the background, as the mountains sloped higher, small houses nestled, smoke rising from every chimney. Christmas decorations adorned doorways and windows and never before or since have I felt the spirit of the season so deeply as I did that snowy night.

The horse clip-clopped its way to my hotel, which lay at the far end of the street. Halfway along, a sign affixed to the side of a building bore the ominous message to the skiers who flocked to the village: "Broken bones repaired here."

When the sleigh stopped in front of my hotel, I looked up for the first time at the huge and gracefully curved Matterhorn rising like a pyramid from the mountains around it. The magnificence of it took my breath away. No wonder it was called "the mountain of mountains!"

I left the sleigh reluctantly to go into the hotel, wanting to stay outside and drink in the beauty that surrounded me. I was reminded of the words of Goethe - he surely must have been here when he wrote them: "I would say to the moment, linger awhile. Thou art so fair."

The hotel was old fashioned, but luxurious, and had been accommodating the public since the last half of the nineteenth century. The reception clerk greeted me and sent me on my way to a spacious room. There was barely enough time to bathe and change for dinner.

When I reached the dining room, the maitre d' escorted me to a table where I had a full view of the room and the other guests. I remember it all so clearly - the colors, the textures, the way it smelled of freshly baked bread and cheese fondue.

Near the entrance the maitre d' stood, overseeing the waiters with stern attention, snapping his fingers when he saw a table that required service, directing the sommelier to a guest who needed advice as to the proper wine to order with his meal, making certain that each diner felt special.

My waiter, Paul, blond and rosy-cheeked, looked about seventeen years old. He obviously took pleasure in his job. We discussed the menu and when I asked his advice about several of the items listed, he stammered and confessed that, in fact, he had started to work only last week.

"My father has been a waiter at this hotel for thirty years and I am following in his footsteps." He glanced with pride at an older man who took care of guests at the other end of the dining room.

I placed my order and Paul left, smiling and bowing.

The sommelier brought a glass of wine and I sipped it and observed the other diners - athletic, vibrant with energy, chic in their stylish apres-ski clothes. At that moment, Paul headed down the center of the dining room with the first course for my table and the others surrounding me. He carried the tray high and stole a quick glance toward his father to see if he was observing him in his important mission. As he looked away, he failed to see that the beautiful carpet underneath had buckled. His effort to keep from falling would have done credit to the world's foremost ice skater in the Olympics. But to no avail.

He stumbled, lurched forward, and finally fell on his face, soup spilling, dousing everyone within ten feet.

The maitre d" stood over him, his expression severe, motioning for a cleanup crew from the kitchen. Paul, prone on the floor, lifted his face from the bowl of soup where it had landed. Some of the vegetables and cheese had stuck to his hair and eyebrows and chin. His wonderful world had ended! I could have cried for him and wished I could have interceded with the maitre d" for mercy, but he seemed to be in no mood for interference. He banished Paul from the dining room with a snap of his fingers and a toss of his head.

I spent the rest of my holiday browsing through the village, making a few purchases from the shopkeepers, walking beside the frozen brook that flowed in warm weather and visiting the quaint Church of St. Maurice nearby. I walked through the cemetery with its graves of many climbers who had met their deaths in the mountains.

I regretted that I did not see Paul again before I left. The staff at the hotel seemed reluctant to discuss the incident with me, a guest.

Twenty-five years later, in the youth of old age, I went back to Switzerland, realizing that this would probably be my last trip to Zermatt. I was anxious to see if it had changed. When I arrived, I was pleasantly surprised. As if held in a delicate suspension of time it was as charming as I remembered it.

Summer is as lovely as December but in a different way – wild flowers, rippling streams and clear blue light. An old-fashioned horse-drawn carriage met me when I arrived. The smell of bratwurst and fondue still permeated the air, this time from the sidewalk cafes. We passed the sign directing skiers with broken bones to the proper door. The Matterhorn gleamed as majestically as ever, the invariable warm welcome was extended when I checked into the hotel. Dusk hovered over the village as I unpacked and dressed for dinner. I headed for the dining room, wondering if I would have the same fascination with this generation of guests in their chic clothes and a domineering maitre'd snapping his fingers at ever obedient waiters.

At the entrance to the elegant dining room memories washed over me. Burgundy velvet curtains framed the windows, crystal chandeliers sparkled overhead, the same maitre d'—no—no, it couldn't be! It wasn't the same maitre d' - it was Paul!

Amazingly, he remembered me. The thought of looking up into my face from the spilled bowl of soup must have seared my features into his memory. The next day we had a lovely visit over a cup of tea in a small private dining room and I told him how many times I had thought of him through the years.

"The episode that night seemed to be the end of my dreams," he said, "My father gave me courage, though, when he told me that a similar incident had occurred to him in his youth. And, finally, the maitre d' found humor in the situation and decided to give me another chance. I learned not to look up when carrying a tray full of soup and now that I am maitre d', I feel sympathetic towards my young waiters." He smiled and we sipped our tea in a spirit of friendship and understanding.

Now that I have reached my final phase - Old Age - I think back of the many things I have learned throughout life. The most meaningful is the realization that there are worlds within worlds far more complex than the ones I had pictured before I came to know the people who live in other lands. Before, I had existed in my own cocoon, my protected bastion, secure from what I perceived to be inconsequential problems in those other worlds.

Why would a falling waiter and a tray of spilled soup in a remote village in Switzerland be of interest to me in my own insulated corner? Because, travel opened small windows for me to see inside those other worlds, to become aware of their peoples, their grief became my sorrow, their laughter my joy, and now I share with them in the larger universe that encompasses us all.

MEET THE JUDGES

Louise Murphy Gearin has been published nationally and internationally. Her publishing credits include *the Journal of Medical Biography, Wild West Magazine, the Cousteau Society's Dolphin Log, Mature Living, Alive!, Mid West Poetry Review* and a number of small literary magazines. She has won numerous awards in fiction, non-fiction and poetry. In 1996 she was elected Poet Laureate of the Poetry Society of Tennessee.

Stephen Malin, poetry judge, has published poetry and articles about poetry and theatre for many years in some of the nation's leading literary journals. Believing the urgency of poetry exists in both its contemplative and its communal aspects, he has also performed verse—his own and others— in a variety of states and stages. He has work in recent or pending issues of *Antioch Review, Beloit Poetry Journal, Sewanee Review* and more.

Tom McDaniel, professionally know as Thomas W. McDaniel, is an attorney in Memphis, TN. He has been President, and is Poet Laureate Emeritus, Life Member and Honorary member of PST. He judged the haiku.

Dorothy Bullard Tacker, Tyronza, AR, judged the humorous poetry. She is an avid reader and has read the published work of her daughter, Frances Cowden, for almost 40 years and including all of the issues of *Grandmother Earth* as well as many issues of *Voices International* and *Tennessee Voices.*

Dr. Malra Treece is Professor Emeritus, College of Business and Economics, University of Memphis. She is author of *April's Father and Other Stories and Poems* as well as thirteen college textbooks including the seventh edition of *Successful Communication in Business and the Profession.* She judged the prose.

MEET THE STAFF

Frances Brinkley Cowden is founder of Grandmother Earth and Life Press. Grandmother Earth won the 1995 Business Environmental Award given by the city of Germantown, TN. Cowden received the Purple Iris Award in 2000 for outstanding contribution to the community through her publishing and the Life Press Writers' Conference. The Iris Awards are co-sponsored by the Memphis Branch of the National Organization of Business Women. In 2001 she was selected as one of the 50 Women who Make a Difference by *Memphis Woman Magazine.*

Frances Darby contributed to *Our Golden Thread,* and has poetry in all of the *Grandmother Earth* series. She is the widow of the late Rev. James W. Darby, a United Methodist minister. She is an editorial assistant for *Grandmother Earth.*

Patricia Smith is editor of and critic for *Grandmother Earth* and other GEC and Life Press publications. Her Life Press Conference workshop has been popular each year with both beginning and seasoned writers. She is an officer of the NLAPW, Chickasaw Branch.

Marcelle Zarshenas Nia, a Memphis attorney, has helped with the editing of Grandmother Earth publications since its beginning in 1993.

CONTRIBUTORS

Common abbreviations used: PST, Poetry Society of Tennessee; NLAPW, National League of American Pen Women; NFSPS, National Federation of State Poetry Societies; PRA, Poets' Roundtable of Arkansas.

Jane E. Allen, Wetumpka, AL, enjoys writing fiction, nonfiction, and poetry—and entering contests. Her works have been included in *Progressive Farmer; Ordinary and*

Sacred As Blood: Alabama Women speak; Grandmother Earth; Tough Times, Strong Women; The Alalitcom; 103; Rosie the Riveter Stories; and *Mystery Time.* Her essay "Playhouses" was recently published in *Delta Quill.* She is a member of NLAPW, Montgomery Branch, Montgomery Press and Authors Club and Alabama Writers Conclave and Women in the Arts (WITA).

Helen Allison, Memphis, TN, is a member of PST, NLAPW, Society of Children's Book Writers and Illustrators. She writes poetry, juveniles, and short stories. Author of ten books she has been widely published and has won numerous awards. She is listed in several *Notable Americans, Who's Who in Poetry,* etc.

Laura Black, Atlanta, GA, is in the MFA-Poetry program at Georgia State University and is also a professional photographer, specializing in children.

Laurie Boulton, Melbourne, FL, [pen name Lauri Silver] BA, M.Ed.; retired. Published in journals and specialized magazines, *Kicker, Grapevine;* newspapers, *Florida Today.* Won several non-fiction short story/essay awards and numerous poetry awards in many states. Her specialty area is photography to illustrate poems for and about veterans. Two photo illustrated books, for and about veterans (free to veterans) Echoes of the Heart for family and friends.

Marcia Camp, Little Rock, AR, is author of You Can't Leave Till You Do the Paperwork. She won the Sybil Nash Abrams award in 1984 and again in 1998. She was recently nominated for the Pushcart Prize.

Bettye Kramer Cannizzo, Decatur, AL, has been published in several journals such as *Grandmother Earth, The Elk River Review, Alalitcom, Alabama Horizons,* and *NFSPS's Anthology.* She has served in several capacities in the Alabama State Poetry Society, the Alabama Conclave of Writers, the Huntsville branch of NLAPW and the Mountain Valley Poets. Bettye is Vice President of the

ASPS and secretary of the Alabama State Association of NLAPW. She has won numerous awards.

Arla Clemons, Las Crosse, WI, is a retired physical education teacher, now pursuing her writing career. She has been published in the *Wisconsin Poets' Calendar, Touchstone, Promise Magazine, Grandmother Earth, Julian's Journal* and *Splintered Sunlight* (Anthology 2000 published by the Arizona State Poetry Society). Grandmother of nine, she grew up on a farm, and writes today of those memories.

John Crawford, Professor of English Literature at Henderson State University, Arkadelphia, AR, is also a noted pianist.

Anna DeMay, Orange Park, FL, is a member of the Florida State Poets Association. Her poems have appeared in literary journals, most recently *Comstock Review* and *Spindrift.*

Michael R. (Mick) Denington, a retired Air Force colonel, writes poetry and fiction. He has won numerous prizes and his works have appeared in local, regional and international publications. He is active in local and state writing organizations, currently serving as President of PST and The Tennessee Writer's Alliance. He serves as director of the United Poets Laureate, International. He and his wife, Marilyn, live in Bartlett, TN.

Frieda Beasley Dorris, Memphis, TN, is one of the originators of the Dorsimbra poetry form. A past president of the Poetry Society of TN, she has won numerous awards for her poetry.

Lenna Reynolds Frye, a registered nurse, and her husband, Merwin, retired from Hutchinson, Kansas to Bella Vista, Arkansas in 2002. Shortly after moving she started drawing and has been encouraged by artists from both Judson Baptist Church and The Village Art Club where she has membership.

Madelyn Eastlund, Beverly Hills, FL, a retired instructor of Fiction Writing and Poetry Writing for Central Florida Community College, and also for Withlacoochee Institute, is in the middle of her sixteenth year as editor of two Verdure Publications magazines: *Poets Forum Magazine; Harp-Strings Poetry Journal.* She is immediate past president of the NFSPS, past president of Florida State Poets Assoc., and is in her 21st year as the Poetry Workshop Director for the Gingerbread Poets. For over forty years her fiction, essays, and poetry have appeared in various magazines, journals, anthologies, and newspapers.

Winifred Hamrick Farrar is Poet Laureate of Mississippi and her work has been widely published. She is a member of the Mississippi Poetry Society, the Poetry Society of Tennessee, and the NLAPW, Chickasaw Branch.

Betty Heidelberger, Lexa, AR, has been published in several literary magazines and has won numerous awards. She lives on a farm near West Helena and part of the time in Sherwood, AR. She was awarded the Merit Award in 1998 from the Poets' Roundtable of AR.

Tana Ford received her B. M. degree in Voice and her B. A. degree in English from Belhaven College in Jackson, MS. She has taught gifted students and worked as a secretary. She has happily retired and works as secretary/jack-of-all trades in her husband's photography business. She has won numerous poetry awards throughout the South and had poems published in several journals including "Lucidity" and "Voices International." A former member of PST, she judged the Poetry Society of Tennessee contest last year.

Betty Gifford, almost native Memphian, transplanted to Denver 14 years ago, widow, 7 children, 17 grandchildren, 16 great-grandchildren, free-lance writer for last 14 years. She has had over 35 magazine articles published.

Isabel Joshlin Glaser, Memphis, TN, is a former teacher. She is a well-published writer of poetry and prose for children and adults. She is author of *Dreams of Glory: Poems Starring Girls* (Atheneum/Simon and Schuster) and Old Visions, New Dreams (Old Hickory Press). She has published in *Cicada, School Magazine, Instructor, Greensboro Review, Mississippi Review, Prairie Schooner, Humpty Dumpty, Explore, Child Life, Cricket, Spider Together,* and many anthologies and textbooks. She won the Memphis Magazine Fiction Prize in 1990 and again in 1992.

Sarah Hull Gurley is a member of PST and was born and reared in Louisiana. Degreed in Business Administration from Louisiana Technical College. Former president and owner of United Warehouse and Terminal Corporation and of The Deliberate Literate, bookstore and cafe. Member of St. Luke's United Methodist Church. Currently residing in Germantown, Tennessee and Leesburg, Florida.

⊠ᦱᦱⓈᦱⓆᦱ ×▤ ▮ᦱⓈᦱⓄᦱ② lives in Benton, TN, on the Big Sandy River from which she obtains inspiration for writing. She teaches second grade at Camden Elementary School and belongs to three writers groups.

Verna Lee Hinegardner, Hot Springs, AR, was Poet Laureate of Arkansas for 13 years. She is past president of the AR Pioneer Branch of NLAPW; Past President of PRA; President of Roundtable Poets of Hot Springs; served 12 years on the board of NFSPS and chaired two of their national conventions; member of Poets' Study Club, Poetry Society of America, International Poetry Society, and is listed in The International Directory of Distinguished Leadership. Hinegardner was inducted into the AR Writers' Hall of Fame in 1991; won their Sybil Nash Abrams Award in 1973, 1979 and 1991; and received the AR Award of Merit in 1976 and 1983; and is the author of eleven books of poetry.

Cornelius Hogenbirk, Waretown, NJ, is a retired sales engineer. His hobbies are photography, gardening, and writing. His writing and photography have been in every issue of *Grandmother Earth*.

Elizabeth Howard, Crossville, TN, is the author of *Anemones,* Grandmother Earth, 1998, which contains poetry that has been previously published in journals and anthologies. She is a frequent award-winner.

Lois Batchelor Howard, Santee, CA, is a graduate of The University of Michigan in Music. She has won dozens of local and national writing competitions. Her poetry, short stories, and articles have been published in the National League of American Pen Woman magazine, POET magazine, The Toledo Blade, the Santa Fe Digest, Grandmother Earth, San Diego City Works, the Florida State Review, and other newspapers and literary journals.

Faye Williams Jones, North Little Rock, AR is a retired school librarian who received numerous awards during her career. She presented workshops at state, regional, national, and international library and media conferences. Memberships include PRA and River Market Poets Branch. Interests are reading, writing, painting, gardening and traveling. She creates handmade books for her award winning poetry.

Anne-Marie Legan, Herrin, IL, received from Cader Publishing, Ltd. the 1998 International Poet Of The Year Chapbook Competition, $5,000 grand prize and publication of *My Soul's On A Journey.* In the last four years, since she first started writing she's won over a hundred awards, winning the "Distinguished Poet's Award," (Sparrowgrass) Editor's Choice Awards, (different magazines) and the President's Award in 1996, 97, 98, 99, 2000 and 2001. Active in Southern IL Writer's Guild, she has been published widely, including seven poetry books and two mystery novels, *Tattoo of a Wolf Spider* and *Deadly Case.*

Madge H. Lewis, Memphis, TN, is a widow, retired owner of a travel agency and has two great-grandchildren. She is an award winner of the Memphis Story-Tellers League.

Ellaraine Lockie, Sunnyvale, CA, has received over 70 poetry awards and her work has appeared in journals, anthologies, magazines, and broadsides in the US and Canada.. Her first collection, *Midlife Muse,* won Poetry Forum's chapbook contest, 2000. Other books include, *All Because of a Button: Folklore, Fact and Fiction,* St. Johann Press, and *Gourmet Papermaker,* Creative Publications (US) and Collins and Brown (England).

Angela Logsdon, Memphis, TN, is a descendant of the Cherokee/Choctaw nations. She strives to reflect the beauty of her heritage in her writing. Her poetry and photography have been previously published in Grandmother Earth. She is a member of PST.

Margo LaGattuta, Rochester, MI, has her MFA in Poetry from Vermont College. Her published books include *Embracing the Fall, The Dream Givers,* and *Diversion Road,* and she has had work published in many national literary magazines and anthologies. She is also an essayist with a weekly column in *Suburban Lifestyles.*

Eileen Malone's most recent first prize awards were from Pen Women's Della Crowder Miller Poetry Prize and Milford Fine Arts Council. She has published in over 400 publications with awards in the *Haight Ashbury Literary Journal* competition and the *Glimmer Train* magazine open poetry contest as well as *Potpourri, Voices International* and Emily Dickinson Awards. Her home is the necropolis of Colma, where San Francisco buries its dead.

David Millison, La Conner, WA, is the husband of poet Marjorie Millison.

Frances W. Muir, Coral Springs, FL, is currently a free-lance writer. Her careers have included teaching, electronics techonology, technical writing, journalism and a stint as a legal secretary.

Anne Norris, Memphis, TN, is a member of Memphis Story Tellers' League. She is the author of *The Charm Bracelet and Other Stories*, a book of short tellable stories, poetry and devotionals.

Rosalyn Ostler, Salt Lake City, UT, has published in *Grandmother Earth, ByLine, Encore, Anthology of New England Writers, Poetry Panorama, Pennsylvania Prize Poems,* etc. She co-authored *By the Throat* and is an officer of the Utah State Poetry Society. She a grandmother and serves in scouting and her church.

Jane Randall, Centerville, UT, is active in The Utah State Poetry Society and League of Utah Writers, having served terms as chapter president in each, and earning a smattering of local, state and national writing awards. Her most gallant accomplishment has been to faithfully keep a gratitude journal, recently noting blessing #14,086 (& counting).

Clovita Rice, Little Rock, AR, edited *Voices International* for 29 years and was a director of the Arkansas Writers Conference is now concentrating on her own poetry and watercolor. Her book of poetry, *Crystal and Creatures,* is being published by Grandmother Earth.

Lucy Ray Roberts, Memphis, TN, has just published her book of poetry and prose, *Gifts: Extraordinaries in an Ordinary Life.*

Rhonda Roberts, is an award winner from Searcy, AR.

LaVonne Schoneman, Seattle, WA, is a former actress. Her husband, children and eight grandchildren also reside in WA. She is author of the popular "How to Cope" series on coping with post-polio, she also writes (and judges) fiction and poetry.

N. Colwell Snell is a native of Wyoming. His poetry has won awards locally and nationally and has been published in several anthologies, including *Byline, Poetry Panorama, Encore, Bay Area Poets Coalition, California Quarterly, Grandmother Earth* and *Anthology Literary Magazine.* He is co-author of *By the Throat, Selected Poems.* He has been featured "In the Spotlight" of *Poet's Forum Magazine.*

Stacy Smith, Anderson, IN, is the editor of *Reflections of Nature: An Anthology of Nature Poems* and *In the Eyes of the Wild: An Anthology of Wildlife Poetry & Short Stories.* Her poetry has also appeared in *The Heron's Nest* haiku journal, *Dream Catcher: Mind Life* by Julianna Smith, 2004 *Angel Datebook,* and on the hood of a non-professional racecar. She co-authored nature poetry chapbook, *Along the River and Through Flowered Fields.*

Marilyn Stacy is Professor Emeritus, Richland College, Dallas. TX. She is a psychotherapist in private practice and is vice-president of the Poetry Society of Texas. She co-authored *Practical Applications of Psychology* and her published work includes short stories and articles, most recently in *Venture Inward.* Her poems have won numerous awards and appear in journals and anthologies including papier-mache press *Generation To Generation* and her books, *Along the Path* and *Dreams.*

Russell Strauss, Memphis, TN, has won numerous awards in the NFSPS contests as well as many state contests. He is a member of the board of PST.

Brett Taylor, Knoxville, TN, is originally from Wartsburg, TN. In addition to *Grandmother Earth,* he has published in *Soul, Fountain, The Nocturnal, Lyric, South by SouthEast, Raw Nervz Haiku, Haiku Headlines, Persimmon, Modern Haiku, Cicada,* and *Cotyledon.* His photo appeared in the Knoxville magazine, *Grumpus.*

Vincent J. Tomeo, Flushing, NY, won honorable mention in the Rainer Maria Rilke International Poetry Competition, 1999. His works appear in anthologies, newspapers, magazines and on the tape, "The Sound of Poetry." He has a publication in Braille, Whispers from the Heart. He presents poetry readings for a variety of organizations.

Charlene Villella, Murray UT, began writing about 20 years ago, and has had numerous poems published in anthologies nationally and internationally, such as Pudding, Mediphors, Wide Open Poetry, and others. She belongs to four poetry groups and was Poet Laureate of Pleasation and Poet Laureate of the Tri-Valley.

Nancy Watts, Ellicott City, MD, is a member of New England Writers Association. Her publications include Kota Press, Small Brushes and a first book of poetry, *Of Ways Of Looking At A Woman,* through Rosecroft Publishing at rosecroftpub@yahoo.com.

Lucille Morgan Wilson, Des Moines, IA, is a farm girl, transplanted to the city many years ago, but with the country still in her bones. She has been editor of *Lyrical Iowa,* the annual anthology of the Iowa Poetry Association for fifteen years, but her greatest pride is six children and twelve grandchildren.

** **

STUDENT CONTRIBUTORS

Thomas Aldridge, a student member of PST and an award winner, was in the 12th Grade at Bolton (TN) High School. He is now attending the University of Memphis.

Patrick Banks, Christina Brooks and **Courtney Cole** were senior art students at Northside High School when they did these illustrations for *The Walking Stick.* Frances Cowden was their art teacher and advisor for the literary magazine.

Whitney Lauren Brinkley, is in the 10th grade at DeSota Central High School in Southhaven, MS. She is the granddaughter of Frances Cowden and has been published in *Grandmother Earth* previously.

Nathan Roberts, Searcy, AR, wrote his story while in the 6th grade at Southwest Middle School.

Christopher (Grade 5) and Courtney Watts (Grade 7) attend Waterlou Elementary and Ellicott Middle school, in Ellicott City, MD.

Elizabeth Young, Bountiful, UT, wrote this poem while in the ninth grade at Mueller Park Jr. High.

Reza Alexander Zarshenas, Memphis, TN, wrote his story for an assignment at Ridgeway High where he is in the 10th grade. Proud mother, Marcelle Nia, sent it to his grandmother, Frances Cowden.

GRANDMOTHER EARTH PUBLICATIONS

Prices quoted include postage and apply only if ordered directly from Grandmother Earth

Abbott, Barbara, *GRANDMOTHER EARTH'S HEALTHY AND WISE COOKBOOK*, 1-884289-13-4. Healthy and easy cooking, but not diet. First layer of fat skimmed from Southern cooking. Optabind binding; $11.

Benedict, Burnette Bolin, *KINSHIP*, 1-884289-08. Lyrical poetry by Knoxville poet. Chapbook, 1995, $6.

Cowden, Frances Brinkley, *VIEW FROM A MISSISSIPPI RIVER COTTON SACK*, 1-884289-03-7. This collection of poetry and short prose emphasizes family values and farm life in Mississippi County, Arkansas and life in Memphis, Tennessee. Cloth, gold imprint, 1993, $15.
TO LOVE A WHALE; 1-884289-06-1. Learn about endangered animals from children and educators.

Children's drawings, poetry and prose, PB (Perfect bound) 1995, $8.

BUTTERFLIES AND UNICORNS, ED 4, 1-884289-04-5 (Cowden and Hatchett) Poetry for the young and young-at-heart with notes on teaching creative writing. PB, 1994, $8.

Daniel, Jack, *SOUTHERN RAILWAY- FROM STEVENSON TO MEMPHIS*—1-884289-17-7. 1/2x 11with 400+ photographs, 360 pages, 1996. Daniel is an Alabama native who now lives in Cordova, TN. Documents and other papers with heavy emphasis upon history of Southern Railway and its workers. PB, $35.

MY RECOLLECTIONS OF CHEROKEE, ALABAMA, 1-884289-25, 8 1/2x11. 300+ photographs of author's family history and life in early Cherokee, 232 pages, PB, 1998, $22.

THOROUGHBREDS OF RAILROADING: YESTERDAY AND TODAY, ISBN 1-884289-26-6 1999, 312 pages, 8 1/2x 11, pictorial history of several railroads. PB, $29.

Hatchett, Eve Braden, *TAKE TIME TO LAUGH*: It's the Music of the Soul. 1- 884289-00-2. Humorous poetry taking off on Eden theme. Chapbook, very limited edition, 1993, $9.

Howard, Elizabeth, *ANEMONES*, 1-884289-27-4, Prize-winning poetry, all previously published, East Tennessee (Crossville) poet, introduction by Connie Green, creative writing instructor, U.T. 1998, $9.

Schirz, Shirley Rounds, *ASHES TO OAK*, 1-884289-07-X Poetry of the lakes region by widely-published Wisconsin author. Grandmother Earth chapbook winner, 1995, $6.

GRANDMOTHER EARTH SERIES: $8 each (multiple copies $7 each, Volume II is $5) Order by Volume number.

GRANDMOTHER EARTH II and III feature Tennessee writers. Volume IV features Arkansas Writers. Volume VII features Alabama writers. Volume VIII features Mississippi writers. Volume IX features Florida writers.

LIFE PRESS PUBLICATIONS

Boren, Blanche S., *THORNS TO VELVET. Devotionals from a Lifetime of Christian Experience.* 1-884289- 231, Blanche S. Boren, Kivar 7, gold imprint, cloth, $18.

Cowden, Frances Brinkley, *OUR GOLDEN THREAD: Dealing with Grief,* 1-884289-10-x, Ed. Personal testimonies and poetry of 40 contributors from clergy and lay writers who deal with different kinds of grief using personal experiences in their faith journeys. Kivar 7 cloth, gold imprint, 1996, $15.

ANGELS MESSENGERS OF LOVE AND GRACE, 1-884289-18-5. True stories of angel experiences by contributors from all walks of life. 96 pages, perfect bound, 1999, $10.

TOWARD IMAGERY AND FORM: A WRITER'S NOTE-BOOK, 1-8884289-29-0. Loose leaf or coil notebook which contains lessons on strengthening writing skills though poetry and prose lessons. Editing, imagery and poetry forms are stressed. Many forms used are explained. Prize-winning examples by contemporary poets. Lessons were from the first five years of Life Press Writers' Association. $10.

Crow, Geraldine Ketchum, BLOOM WHERE YOU ARE TRANSPLANTED, 1-884289-12-6. A resident of Little Rock, Arkansas, Crow grew up in Hot Springs and tells of life in Perry County where she and her husband farmed for several years. Humorous, inspirational approach about moving from the city to the country. PB, 1996, $10.

Davis, Elaine Nunnally, *MOTHERS OF JESUS: FROM MATTHEW'S GENEALOGY,* 1-884289-05-3. Biography of five women mentioned in Matthew. 344 pp. PB, 1994, $11.
EVES FRUIT, 1-884289-11-8, Defense of Eve and implications for the modern woman. PB, 1995, $10.

PATRONS

The eighth annual

Life Press Christian Writers' Conference (and national contest) will be held in August, 2005 in Memphis, Tennessee. Write P. O. Box 2018, Cordova, TN 38088 for more information or download from www.grandmotherearth.com. **This conference is of interest to both beginning and seasoned writers.**

A SPECIAL THANK YOU TO

Frances Darby and Lorraine Smith

For their faithful service
as editorial assistants.
Due to circumstances
they both have had to leave
our staff.
We appreciate all
you have done
throughout the years.

Love and Prayers,
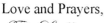

Memorials

Rev, Archie Clifford Morrison
Wife of Alice Morrison
January, 1925—October 22, 2003

Ruth Wylie Boyd Pell
Mother of Elizabeth Pell
April 13, 1901—June 27, 2004

Helen Irene Forrester
Mother of Willis R. Forrester
October 25, 1925—August 2, 2004

Mary Lourine White
Mother of Stephen Edward White
January 19, 1917—October 12, 2004

***

The Poetry Society of Tennessee morns the
loss of our members

James Clifford Middleton
May 14, 1920—September 2003

Sibyl M. Grammer
October 8, 1915—July 1, 2004

Sami Morris Sax
April 29, 1942—July 1, 2004

INDEX